UE IT! DRAW

BUILD IT!

I ♥ YOU

BAKE IT!

'CIL IT! DO IT!

IT!

May 1999
Washington County Library
Woodbury, MN 55125

Mary Engelbreit's
WINTER

Mary Engelbreit's

WINTER

CRAFT BOOK

Illustrated by Mary Engelbreit
Written by Charlotte Lyons
Photography by Barbara Elliott Martin

ANDREWS AND McMEEL
A Universal Press Syndicate Company
Kansas City

is a registered trademark of
Mary Engelbreit Enterprises, Inc.

10 9 8 7 6 5 4

Library of Congress Cataloging-in-Publication Data

Engelbreit, Mary.
    [Winter craft book]
    Mary Engelbreit's winter craft book / illustrated by Mary Engelbreit ; written by Charlotte Lyons ; photography by Barbara Elliott Martin.
       p. cm.
    Includes index.
    ISBN 0-8362-2231-8 (hd)
    1. Holiday decorations. 2. Handicraft. 3. Holiday cookery. 4. Cookery. I. Lyons, Charlotte. II. Title.
TT900.H6E55 1996
745.594'1-dc20
                                     96-11117
                                         CIP

Design by Stephanie Raaf

Contents

IT IS A FINE SEASONING
FOR JOY✻TO THINK
OF THOSE WE LOVE..
·MOLIERE·

one.
CHRISTMAS

Father Christmas

*Christmas is a cherished time
for those who create enchanted memories
for family and friends.*

Little arrangements all over the house make the most of decorating themes, but the fireplace is often the favorite focus. This year, surprise everyone with a Father Christmas built with a scarecrow body and a painted papier mâché face. An oversized overcoat, corded belt, and gloves cover his plump pillowy shape, along with a big woolen hood and frothy beard made from quilt batting. His bundled pack made from a tablecloth is chock full of wrapped Christmas gifts and treats to inspire everyone's fondest holiday dreams.

Potted Trees

*Make these little holiday trees
for yourself and your friends.*

Styrofoam cones are spiked on painted wooden dowels planted into little pots filled with floral clay. Before assembling, wrap the trees in fabric, ribbon, or paper and then decorate each with buttons, beads, and braids. One tree has brightly colored beads threaded onto ribbon that cascades from the top; another has button flowers pinned onto a black felt wrapping. Painted pots or little jars found around the house make simple bases. When set together with other favorite Christmas decorations, they brighten a tabletop scene.

Ginger Man Tree

*Store-bought cookies sweeten the simple charm
of a craft tree adorned with the little men
dressed up in buttons and bows.*

Use a hot-glue gun to attach small bow ties
and loop hangers made with plaid gift ribbon. A handful of unmatched shirt buttons gives
each its own holiday look. The angel wings and dress
are easy to make from paper doilies pinched and
glued to the back or cut to fit the front, while four
overlapping buttons make a halo. Glue the extra
cookies around the base like little paper dolls hold-
ing hands. A garland of red beads or a cranberry
string is all that is needed to complete this dear
kitchen tree.

Class-ic Wreath

*Create a gift for your child's teacher
that she will treasure this year and always.*

Ask each child to contribute a wallet-size school picture from picture day. Cut each shining face to fit into big dress buttons that make perfect frames. An assortment of charms and trinkets found at the craft store (or in the desk) adds touches of whimsy. Simply glue the framed faces and decorations onto a small silk wreath and add a ribbon. The eraser at the top of the ribbon holds a hook with a screw to anchor the entire wreath.

A+!

Pancake Basket

*A simple gift for a friend combines
a gingham sack full of homemade pancake mix
with a bottle of pure maple syrup
in a basket sprigged with an ornament
and recipe notecard.*

To make Pancake Mix:

3 cups flour

1 tablespoon double-acting baking powder

1 tablespoon sugar

To make pancakes, combine in a bowl 1 cup of mix, 1 cup of milk, 1 egg and 1 tablespoon oil. Mix with a wooden spoon. Drop spoonfuls onto a hot, seasoned griddle. Flip when most of the bubbles burst, cook 30 seconds more, and serve. Makes twelve, 4-inch pancakes.

Button Collage Pins

*Stickers or cutouts become whimsical
character pins when you apply them
to matboard backs and then add
fancy buttons and charms.*

Trace the sticker shape onto the matboard or cardboard and cut out with an X-acto® knife. Glue the sticker onto the custom-made backing and then hot-glue extras into place. All that's left is to glue a pinback onto the back. For a crafty friend, make one pin and present it in a boxful of clever materials so she can make more of her own.

christmas

ut far more bright
More dear than all
That dream of home
That dream of home

Fancy Pocket

*These slim pocket bags make the most of
cherished snippets just big enough
for eyeglasses or a lipstick and comb.*

Splendid vintage fabrics are easy to collect, but they usually can be found only in small amounts. Cut the fabric into two rectangles. Place the right sides together and sew on three sides. Turn and finish the top edge by hand. Add lovely cording and trimmings like tassels and cut-glass buttons for beautiful evening bags. These can be put together in an afternoon. And wouldn't one also make an exquisite wrap for a small gift?

Snowmen Cutouts

*If you've planned a party for your holiday,
consider making these silly snowmen cutouts
for your guests to enjoy.*

Cut oversized snowmen shapes from panels of
foamcore and decorate them with markers.
Attach them to the backs of kitchen chairs so that
little ones can use the chair to reach the cutout
faces. Have several disposable cameras on hand and
let the frolic begin. Besides filling an album with
great snapshots from the party, you might also create your own holiday card for next year.

Snowball Tree

Twilight brings magic to a favorite corner
capturing the wonder and merriment
of a child's Christmas dream.

An evergreen is simply trimmed with snowballs fashioned from strips of quilt batting. Rolled rag-style, they can be put together in no time at all. Holiday postcards and plastic icicles contribute their charm and, at the base, a little red fence filled with batting scraps anchors the snowy scene. Stand-up snowmen and a shadowbox full of collectible Frostys lend the enchantment of a toy shop window.

Paper Scotty Ornament

Decorations made at home
with everyday materials make the kitchen table
a family workshop.

Draw a simple heart on a piece of oak tag paper or a manilla folder. Inside the heart use markers to draw a scotty, or some other image you love, and then decorate the border with dots and dashes. Cut out the heart and trace it onto a piece of newsprint. Draw a ruffled border that is larger than the first heart and cut it out. Repeat this for the third heart on a piece of red construction paper. Paste all three layers together and make a thread hanger. Make these to use as gift tags or ornaments. They will be remembered in years to come for the spontaneous fun they inspired.

WE SHALL LIGHT A CANDLE OF UNDERSTANDING IN OUR HEARTS WHICH SHALL NOT BE PUT OUT.

two.
HANUKKAH

Hanukkah Gift Wrap

Brightly colored tissue paper makes a festive bow for a gift wrap.

Cut twenty 6" x 6" squares of different colored papers. Pinch each in the center to form a bow-tie shape and stack them, securing the stack with a ribbon tie. Fluff the paper layers until all the colors stand up and show like flower petals. Tie the bow to the top of a gift that has been wrapped in matching colored paper and fill the center of the bow with candy gold coins. Hot-glue these and others to the package. You can be sure that your gift will be opened first.

Menorah

The time spent building this menorah with your children will make it one of your family's favorite heirlooms.

Begin with a woodscrap, such as the one shown—a 2x2 that is about 21" long. Paint it a bright color and decorate one side with a checkerboard if you like. Purchase and paint nine wooden candle holders in a variety of patterns and colors. Seal the paint with an acrylic sealer that gives it a shiny, durable finish. Using an assortment of wooden beads in different colors, stack the beads and candleholders to achieve the staggered heights shown. The center candle is traditionally taller than the others. Glue all the pieces into place including four large beads for feet. Fill with candles and celebrate!

hanukkah

NEW YEAR'S
three.

New Year's Invitation

For New Year's, take some time to make individual invitations for a small and elegant dinner party.

D ecorated papers from the stationery shop can be combined with charms and paper or fabric cutouts to create an extraordinary invitation worth framing. This one actually shows a place setting on a placemat. Sew to backing paper along one edge, allowing it to open like a book. Write your message or invitation inside. Hand-deliver this wrapped as a gift—which is, indeed, just what it is.

Evening Bag

*A lovely evening bag is a stunning accessory
for a New Year's outing.*

Purchase a pattern for a simple evening bag sewing project. Use velvet or brocade to make an especially lovely purse. Gold cording and a glittering tassle add dressy sparkle.

New Year's Table

For a formal evening, set your party table with simple sophistication and style.

A gilded birdcage (using gold spray paint) encloses nests of moss and topiaries with a little bird on the perch. Dime store goblet stems are dressed up with gold rickrack entwined around sprigs of dried blooms and silk leaves. Plain white napkins with added button holes and fancy dress buttons (or cuff links) enhance the romantic setting along with vintage trays appearing as place mats. Finishing touches such as gold-rimmed china and candlelight complete the scene, setting the mood of casual elegance.

Hors d'Oeuvre

*Make this elegant,
but easy New Year's hors d'oeuvre
using a variety of simple ingredients.*

2 packages frozen puff pastry dough
2 packages boursin cheese
Heavy cream
Toppings of your choice described below

Defrost puff pastry according to directions. Roll out slightly with a rolling pin. Cut out stars and moons with a cookie cutter. Bake at 400 degrees until puffed and golden. Remove from oven, cool, and cut each shape in half to make two layers. Whip boursin with a little cream until it will spread easily. Divide cream mixture into four parts. Mix chopped sundried tomatoes in oil with one batch, pesto with

another, Greek olives with the third, and keep the fourth plain. Spread on pastries and top with your choices of: smoked salmon, capers, and a dab of sour cream and dill; cooked and peeled shrimp with strips of green bean and red pepper with chive; blanched snow peas with red pepper garnish; roast beef with parsley, green peppercorns and a dab of sour cream; or fresh mushrooms sautéed lightly and sprinkled with parsley.

TO KNOW IS NOTHING AT ALL; TO IMAGINE IS EVERYTHING.

ANATOLE FRANCE THIBAULT

CABIN FEVER

four.

Teapot Birdfeeder

When winter settles in, it tucks us away indoors
with time on our hands
and the itch to make the most of it.

A thrift shop coffeepot makes a quick and cute birdfeeder when a window is cut out on each side. Drill a starter hole to begin the cut and then use a jigsaw fitted with a blade that cuts metal. Spoons and forks are bent and superglued into the pot so that they provide perches for visiting birds. Superglue the lid into place permanently and screw in three lengths of chain to hang it from. All that's left to do is fill the pot with your favorite birdseed and hang it from a tree where you can watch the birds enjoy your effort.

Checkerboard

A homemade checkerboard painted up with the colors and flowers of summer brightens any winter day and creates fun to share with the family.

C ut a board and finish the edges or buy a crafter's wood panel big enough to accommodate the 64 squares of a checkerboard. Mark it out and paint the pattern leaving room for a border of simple flowers and leaves. Glue felt onto the back to protect the tabletop and wood finish underneath. Attach two handles to make it easy to move when the table calls for something else. Big shiny dress buttons in two colors make game pieces. Sew up a matching drawstring bag to keep the buttons in when the game is over.

cabin fever

Hats and Scarves

*While you're at the thrift shop,
pick up some colorful knitted sweaters
and transform them
into new woolies for outdoor play.*

Choose acrylic knits that can be washed and dried first. To make a cap, cut a sleeve off at the shoulder and cut again to make a 10" tube. From the inside draw the open top closed with a length of yarn and a running stitch. Roll the hem into a band for the bottom of the cap and sew with a loose hem stitch. Decorate the front with a duplicate stitch or an appliqué cut out from another sweater. The scarf uses the rest of the sweater cut into squares and blanket-stitched together in a patchwork. A length of flannel makes a strong lining—and a warmer scarf!

cabin fever

Dutch Baby

Cold mornings and sleepy heads will rise and shine for this cozy breakfast pancake.

Preheat the oven to 425 degrees. Place a half-stick of butter in a 10" cast-iron ovenproof skillet or heavy baking dish. Put the skillet in the oven while you prepare the batter. In the blender, blend 3 eggs until foamy. Add 3/4 cup milk, 3/4 cup flour, 1/4 teaspoon salt and 1/4 teaspoon vanilla. Blend only to combine. When the butter is melted (but before it burns), remove the hot skillet and roll it so that the butter evenly greases the pan. Immediately pour the batter into the hot pan and return to the hot oven. Bake for 25 minutes until puffed and golden. Serve in wedges with slices of lemon, pats of butter, and powdered sugar that melt together to make a lemony syrup. Serves 2-4.

cabin fever

five.
VALENTINE'S

Valentine Wreath

Thank heavens for Valentine's Day!
It comes when we've just about run out
of patience for winter, but it always inspires
the best "make and do" projects
at home to celebrate those we love.

A grapevine wreath inspires the heart with a collection of vintage valentines attached here and there with teacher's putty. Silk flowers and charms fill in the spaces between fond and heartfelt wishes of long ago. If you collect cards from several holidays, simply rotate the cards, decorations, and colored ribbon bows for each holiday.

Valentine Box

*The fun of making a valentine box
is a fond childhood memory for many.*

Make this box as a party centerpiece full of Valentine treats and treasures. A crafter's paper box painted red is trimmed with strips of ribbon and red buttons glued edge-to-edge all around. One precious valentine sits center-stage among white dots of paint. Heart-sprigged handkerchiefs gathered year-round at garage sales add the perfect holiday touch and await all the sweethearts who drop by to celebrate the holiday. Serve sugared shortbread hearts and tea.

Hearty Breakfast

*Treat your real-life valentine
to a romantic breakfast.*

A table set with sweet things includes decoupaged glasses, a heart-shaped topiary of roses, and second-hand chairs decorated with Victorian sentiments. Cook up something sweet like a Dutch Baby (featured on page 52) and enjoy a cozy winter morning with your valentine.

Hearts Galore

*For the holiday, create an arrangement
that makes the most of your favorite things
and enjoy all the fun that comes with collecting.*

Collecting valentine things is easy if you keep your eye open year-round. Hearts appear in many collectibles that are not intended only for valentines. Little heart boxes can accumulate quickly and mix in with other sentimental curios like doll chairs and valentines from other generations. Choose a special spot such as a mantel that you can devote to a cluster of sweethearts and then experiment with arrangements that showcase your treasures.

Sweetheart Mirror

*For a guest room or a teenaged daughter,
make a dressing table mirror
from three decorator shutters.*

Painted pink and white (or any colors you
choose) with a repeating pattern, these window
shutters make perfect frames for mirrors. Hinge
with leather strips cut from an old belt and nailed to
the shutter backs so that the mirror folds in an
adjustable formation and stands alone.

Cherry Fold-up

Make this easy dessert for your valentine.

Combine 1-1/2 cups flour with 1/4 teaspoon salt, 5 tablespoons cold butter, and 4 tablespoons shortening. Use a pastry blender to mix until the butter is broken down into pea-sized bits. Add 4 tablespoons iced water and draw together with a fork into a ball. Chill. On a floured board, roll out the dough to a rough circle several inches larger than the pie pan or baking dish. Transfer gently to the pan. Drain one 16-ounce can of tart cherries packed in water. Mound the cherries in the center of the pastry. Sprinkle with 1/4 cup of sugar and 1/4 teaspoon of almond extract. Fold the remaining pastry up over the mound loosely. Sprinkle again with 1 tablespoon sugar. Bake at 425 degrees for 35–45 minutes until brown. Serves 4.

Heartfelt Sachets

*Stitch up a batch of fragrant sachets
for valentine gifts.*

F elt appliqués are especially fun, but any scrap of fabric sewn into a heart shape and stuffed with lavender, rose petals, or even fresh basil will do. Ruffles and rickrack make fine trimmings along with bits of lace or pieces of handwork that you've saved for something special. Make paper hearts for gift tags and tuck them into secret drawers for valentine surprises.

ST. six. PATRICK'S

Shamrock Pillow

For Saint Patrick's Day, cut and patch vintage linens into a shamrock pillow.

B egin with a pattern that you've made using newspaper. Cut and piece your linens together to form your patchwork shape. Cut another shamrock from green and white gingham or from a linen scrap to fit the patchwork front. With the right sides together, stitch around the edges leaving a small opening for turning and stuffing the pillow. If you like, trim the edges with green ball fringe. This is a comfy holiday decoration on a window seat or bench set with tea-time accessories. Winter is on its way out soon; the green of spring is suddenly everywhere.

st. patrick's

Green & Gold Soup

*For a cozy winter supper anytime,
but especially on St. Pat's Day,
try this simple vegetable soup
that's easy enough for the children to make.*

Combine in a large pot: 6 cups water, 5 chicken bouillon cubes, 5 small red potatoes quartered, and 1 onion. Simmer these ingredients until the potatoes are almost tender. Add 3 handfuls of frozen peas, 3 handfuls of frozen corn, 2 cut up broccoli stalks, 1/2 teaspoon dried marjoram, 1/2 teaspoon dried thyme and 1/2 cup chopped parsley. Simmer a few minutes more and then serve as the main course in big soup bowls. While the soup is simmering, use your favorite biscuit mix to make shamrock-shaped biscuits.

Contributors

Project Designs

Mary Engelbreit: Ginger Man Tree, Class-ic Wreath,
Snowmen Cutouts, Snowball Tree, Checkerboard,
Teapot Birdfeeder, Valentine Box, Hearty Breakfast,
Hearts Galore, Shamrock Pillow

Charlotte Lyons: Potted Trees, Ginger Man Tree,
Pancake Breakfast, Paper Scotty Ornament,
Hanukkah Gift Wrap, Menorah, New Year's Invitation,
New Year's Table, Hats and Scarves, Dutch Baby,
Valentine Wreath, Sweetheart Mirror, Cherry Fold-up,
Heartfelt Sachets

Nicki Dwyer: Evening Bag, New Year's Hors d'Oeuvre,
Green and Gold Soup

Project Designs-continued

Kathy Gillespie: Fancy Pocket

Pat Reed: Button Collage Pins

Joseph Slattery: Class-ic Wreath, Snowmen Cutouts, New Year's Table

Sally Weaver: Father Christmas

Grateful Appreciation to

New City School, St. Louis, Missouri
Kate and Guy Gangi
Molly and Michael Salisbury
Jerry and Betty Scanlon
Stanley Paul
Louise and Taylor Matthews
Judith Combs
Andy Wiltse
Jean Lowe, Stephanie Raaf, Stephanie Barken,
and **Dave Bari**

Index